EARTH TIDES

EARTH TIDES

A COLLECTION OF POETRY

BY

AMY ELIZABETH VAUGHN

2023

TO MY COVEN,
you know who you are.

EARTH TIDES
noun

Earth tide, deformation of the solid Earth as it rotates within the gravitational fields of the Sun and Moon. Earth tides are similar to ocean tides. The Earth deforms because it has a certain degree of elasticity; were it perfectly rigid, there would be no Earth tide.

– ENCYCLOPEDIA BRITANNICA.

TABLE OF ~~ELEMENTS~~

CONTENTS

AIR

with the heat comes the past 6
a pink (full) moon delirium 9
bond 10
a bit of advice 11
lady macbeth 12
my recent google searches 13
or have we eaten on the insane root 14
that takes the reason prisoner— 14
dreamworld 15
dusk 16
i carry within me 17
muse 18
i'll live a lush life 21
lord, what fools these mortals be 22
disconnect 23
sage 24
when you ask me why i write poetry 25
spellcast 26
poconos mornings 27
vision of the future 28
the creative process 29
when the world becomes too much, ... 30
when i'm in the clouds, i'm closer to home 31
a blazing bolt   cracks 32
free writing 33
i'm in love with april showers 34

WATER

aurora's hour . . . . ~~ELEMENTS~~ 40
for my— 41

i'm a faltering flame, fighting eternal sleep. 42
i fill up flimsy papers with sprinkles. 43
the world burns 44
poetry saves me;. 47
disassociation (at its finest) 48
text back days later 49
lost soul (reward: life of contentment) 50
happy new year. 53
in my starless hour 54
heaviness settles softly. 55
black ink pours from my eyes. 56
i am raw 57
grief 58
6am & gloomy 59
vulnerability 60
on hard days the birds help 61
i am tired of the ache 62
i am the castaway 65
anxiety builds like lava 67
(i am safe) 68
    FIRE
oh, to love such a man— 74
your fingers trail my naked back 75
mirage. 76
david. 77
our shadows kiss in golden hour glow. 78
you are light. 81
the truth about us. 82
if you mean it. 83
i am one who loved not wisely but too well 84
i love how your presence brings me peace 85
deportación. 86
candlelight flickers like fairy wings. 87

casanova (or perhaps, narcissus) 88
like spotting. 89
you ask me about my first love 90
like a bedraggled sailor 91
zen connection grounds us together. 92
i am sorry i am not her 93
i am sorry i am not her (part ii). 94
during the dark years, ... 95
union, new jersey. 96
don't think you're special 99
i am the lover in your dreams 100
aries 101
conjuring 102
sunday at the beach. 103
truth is, i miss you 104
will you miss me when i'm gone?. 106
my mouth split open. 107
cursive pirouettes. 108
as i lie upon your chest, ... 109
maybe in another lifetime. 110
maybe in another lifetime (part ii). 113
   EARTH
at some point along the way. 118
an angel eavesdrops on my springtide dreams 119
please don't make this poem about you 120
everyone brave is forgiven 123
temporary highs. 124
all my friends are having babies 126
child of earth 128
meditative spaces 129
i create worlds within me 130
rituals 131
flurries flutter like fairies 132

i could do this for the rest of my life. 135
between storm breaks, we tremble.. 136
doubt 137
a woman's first mistake is putting herself second 138
in between then and now 139
divine goddess—how? 140
aurora. 143
grieving on a sunny day. 144
legacy 145
i need to sit in the rawness 146
you see, i'm a Holy Woman 147
eden's tree 148
    SPIRIT
reincarnation. 155
    acknowledgements 159
    about the author 161

EARTH TIDES

AIR

air

when i was a young girl, i dreamt i was flying over an ancient empire, a city of gold and crystals and pyramids bathed in our star's early hour glow. as the baby yellow sunrise peeked over the horizon, the sky melted into delicious corals and apricots. in my dream, the sky was my home, but earth held me close. when i woke, i ached to fly, to press my palm to tree and show our world how humanity is one with earth and all its tides.

so i flew the only way my soul knew how. through sticky fingers smearing paint onto pages. through reciting the ancient bards as i ran barefoot in dawn's grass. playing with words until magic erupted from my lips. my spirit guides and their folklore gifted this creativity on my breath. my very being coursed with their divinity. my soul's light flickers through expression, eternally.

my coveted sky holds majestic air, our first blessing as we stumble into our earthly bodies. our first precious taste of breath, life, mortality. we work with air, daily – our soul's sacred instrument, the windpipe, births songs. prayers. opinions. spells. art.

air is centering. our nervous systems orient themselves with precious breathwork. my lungs are drunk off the luxurious gas which grows my limbs and allows my soul to get back into creative spaces.

i inhale. exhale. go blank until all i see is sky. here, i greet the little me who wanted to teach everyone to fly. she holds my hand as we breathe our way into a work of art that satisfies us.

i am happiest here – breathing, living, painting poetry.

the wind hears my dream. she steals my voice,
and carries it across lands,
    turns it into birdsong.

WITH THE HEAT COMES THE PAST

summer, swollen and ripe,
barges in like a pregnant woman,
stomach first and out of breath.

summer's kiss, steamy and wet,
trickles down my neck like the Nile—
its salty perfume cracks open memory lane
like an eggshell's sharp shatter on the floor,
spilling faces and places, drenched
in humidity's haze, all over my soul

my younger self dashes by, wilderness in her eyes
sunscreen streaks spread like warpaint
across her nimble body, feet rosy and numb
running on earth's searing sandy cheek
then *boom*—
she baptizes herself in the sea

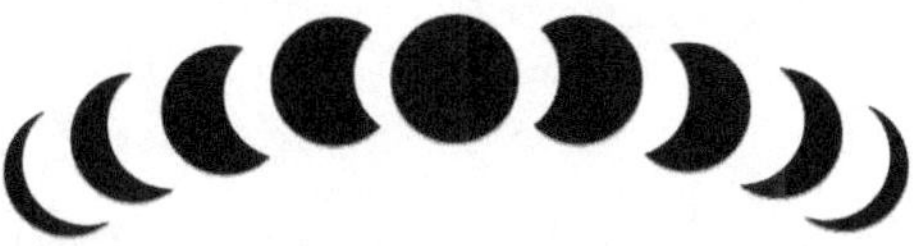

A PINK (FULL) MOON DELIRIUM

it's a full moon again. my soul reverberates with its calling
before my mind remembers. i am lighter than usual. weightless
like soft pinky bubbles, so i rise and walk on clouds sprinkling
purple rainstorms. i fly and roll and languish in strange starlight.
and yet this lightness fizzles and sparks, and an urge to dance
thunders through my veins, too.
how am i both weightless and burning?

miss moon's charge brews love potions in my stomach.
i want to circle fire, to show my moon my bare neck as i lean
back in bliss. i fall with the rain and fall into warm tides.
i swim for eons until my limbs dissolve in the moonlight,
become pearls in oysters.

i am in the ocean floor and the clouds
and i am birthed in fire.
i am everything and nothing at once.
i am me and i am you and i am us.

BOND

if a room was silent enough,
you'd notice our hearts beat in sync.
trauma etched itself in a childlike scrawl
across our flesh in bloody ink.

a bit of advice

meet adam's eyes and ravage the apple with your fangs,
let the juice drip down your cleavage like summer sweat;
find emerald, green grass, graze your naked feet against
its soft touch until your eyes roll back – listen to the wind
whisper morning's secrets, tilt your face up to drink from
the sun; they call us humans, they call us animals, but
we are gorgeous, growing, worrying plants made from
fizzy comet dust and neurons—

a bit of advice

stuff messy, cherry pie in ego's fussy face;
soothe the sick childhood demons terrorizing your ear;
eye the pain lurking in your irises, remove their grasp
from life's ancient steering wheel; open the velvet
curtain in your mind, step into nirvana's violet, starry space
and bathe your soul in its endless white, beaming light—

a bit of advice

hold grace in the palm of your heart like a delicate dietes;
press love into earth with each fumbling footprint;
dig up the roots of peace to plant in your soul,
remember there's beauty in the temporary,
authentic existence is our only goal.

LADY MACBETH

i am soaked in sadness
a red cherry drenched in raging rum
put me in your mouth
tie my stem with your tongue

drupe drips my despair
sticky sugar, key lime and sea salt
saturates your bloodstream
stains your throat until the only
words you speak taste of me

some call it spells
others call it poison
i christen thee devotion

MY RECENT GOOGLE SEARCHES
after @medhaawrites

how to lucid dream. why does a calathea plant stand up at night. flower that symbolizes death. is it a sign that calathea plants are known as "prayer plants." how many bananas equal an egg substitute when making pancakes. what is a sign from the universe vs. wishful thinking. meaning behind the movie NOPE. did i dream about him because i miss him or did something trigger me. navy UFO clip. can you be in therapy your whole life. a recipe containing lemons and zucchini and chicken. how often do my cat's nails need to be trimmed. guided morning meditations. what heals the ache in your chest. why do our emotions hurt physically. disassociation and memory loss. are angel numbers real. why do i keep seeing 222 if i feel so out of alignment. is it normal to wonder how someone from your past is doing. is there a name for the sensation that you've lived a million lives in one. do we shed parts of our consciousness as we evolve. how long does it take to forget someone. do we love people forever. why do i break out more in the summer. what is the longest recorded heat wave in history. will the world end in my lifetime. flights to barbados. flights to ireland. can my cat live forever. are spirits real. does my grandmother know what alzheimer's is doing to her. is alzheimer's genetic. does the soul have memory. how to communicate with the dead. stories of reincarnation. what are souls made of. how to find peace. how to hold on to it.

OR HAVE WE EATEN ON THE INSANE ROOT
THAT TAKES THE REASON PRISONER—

eve's apple reeks of every ignored *no*
and tumbles from my palm
a woman's curse kissing earth

ravaged land bakes in poppy red blood
under the unforgiving sun
we cry to the sky for reprieve
devilish children
unsure of what we've done

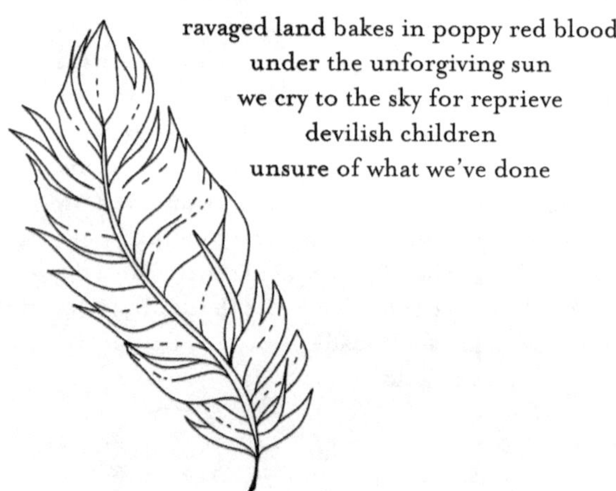

DREAMWORLD

holy silence hugs us as fairy dust cascades from the stars.
i stick my tongue out to taste heaven—the sharp, savory iciness
reminding me of you.
midnight murmurs *sleep well* before three am stumbles in for
their shift.
still, my heart calls for you—
my birdsong echoes through winter's sugar din, ricochets off
rainbows embedded in frozen crystals, settles in your chest.
gives birth to a nagging feeling you've forgotten something.
like the stove's still on, you may have forgotten to feed the cat,
you may have forgotten an entire life before this.
before *this.*
you fall into purple snowbanks, comforted by a protective cold,
enveloped in winter's sweet embrace.
i stand atop the highest mountain you have ever seen—
i reach for you.
i call your first name, from our earliest lifetime.
spellbound, you taste citrus and coppery blood.
oh, how i missed you.
lightning cracks and you awaken.
you hear the call; you know it.
an ancient desire for *before* blooms in your stomach.
you smell the sediment and sea of your first earthbound life.
you hear my laugh in the wind, you kiss snowflakes off my
lashes, you feel my blood's heat.

a bird calls. light bleeds across the horizon. you blink, blink,
blink.

you tell anyone who will listen—
last night, i had the most beautiful dream.

DUSK

i look to the heavens
trace my gaze down orion's belt
wonder which star you call home
countdown the hours
until holy reunion

you swear we'll find each other
under the stirring pink sky
after mother moon murmurs *sweet dreams*
before birds coo morning mantras

- t h e i n - b e t w e e n -

where hands reach
through tangerine clouds
caress the other's ghostly face
this is where you promised
we'll be whole again,
in your divine embrace.

I CARRY WITHIN ME

the desire to fly among angels / the silky sweet honey of your words / demons who cackle in far echoes of my mind / every forgotten lover's breath / recipes for coffee cake and blueberry smoothies / my grandmother's protective prayers / the sound of a 1970s Tootsie pop jingle / a soul dipped in holy water / muscle memory rolling raw papers into flawless cannabis cones / the spells of my ancestors / the ache for Christmas morning in my childhood home / deep starry rivers that stream through my veins / a woman's fear of being a man's prey / Beethoven's sonatas and Picasso's *Les Demoiselles d'Avignon* / rejections transfigured into lessons / the loss of a miracle / Shakespeare's *Puck* and Carroll's *Alice* / ghostly winds from the Highlands / residue of red wine and fairy dust / a battered heart / a soul whose favorite lullaby is the sky's soothing tears / a fear of suffering so potent i reek of it / a frightening voice that coos *you will drown in despair* / the fiery rebirth of a phoenix / an inner goddess who reminds me i like being me / an earthquake of loneliness / a crater deep void impossible to fill / the call to write, always write / and you—always you.

MUSE

the ghosts
   have gone home,
but you—
     you linger.

you leisure in the lobby
of my mind, rest against
the art deco wall
titled c r e a t i v i t y
like you have
all the time
in the world
to breathe in
the sight of me,
scalding my skin,
reminding me
the soul is meant
to ignite like celestials.

where were you, i pen,
i've been waiting lifetimes.

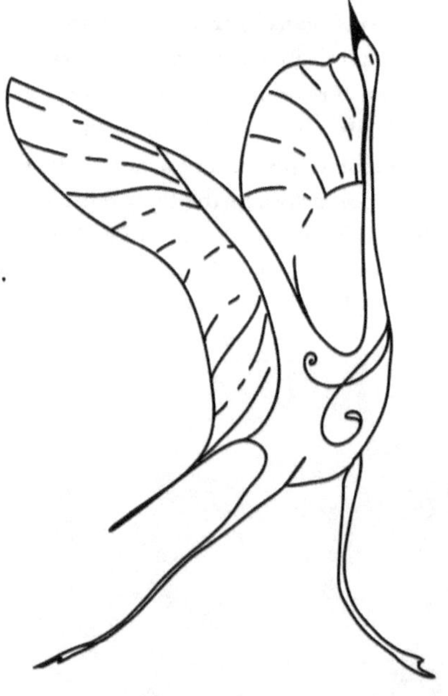

i'll live a lush life
allow rainwater to bathe
my supple skin, detox my soul
start the wee hours of the morning
time traveling through worn pages of fiction
cross my legs, burn sage until it's blackened
meditate until the sun reaches its peak
soak in a lavender bath around noon
with winter's icy rays reflecting wet limbs
tea with poetry will follow
a stroll through the gardens and
a crackling fire with winter pine candles
when an afternoon rain titters in
cat nap under cashmere blankets
and hot soup for dinner—
your arms cocoon me as i sleep
your kiss awakens me from
soft cloudy dreams
i fall in quiet, fervent love

LORD, WHAT FOOLS THESE MORTALS BE

black cracks of lightning permeate the sky
slice zeus's masterpiece into tiny shards of puzzle pieces
the world gasps in raven-purple light
here i cannot help but murmur, *there She is—*

bloody human sin seeps into our earth
rots fungus, poisons our trees, leaks deceit
into our rivers until murky waters clog our throats

every right violated, every atrocity
exhales its stank breath and suffocates us—
every act of hate coils in molten lava
releases acidic steam from our eyes

we beg, *we have lost our way.*
   —have m e r c y on our souls—
we whisper to our gods and sin again
until our self-proclaimed holy days trundle by
we preach, preach, preach and
      forget to listen

DISCONNECT

i look in the mirror at this being
that is my body and wonder what my soul
looks like without it

i try to remember the Before
before i came to earth
before i was in my mother's womb
before i heard her heartbeat
and realized i'd landed safely

i dream i shift like a kaleidoscope
i'm shades of baby yellows and pastel blues
rich purples and never-ending black
cracks of vibrant oranges
strokes of soft greens

small yet infinite
lost yet so loved

SAGE

a single lit match kisses
sacred dried herbs
grown from the garden
under the harvest moon
and my old soul sighs in relief
of ancient practice

releasing pain
through the flame
i watch my spirit guides
blacken the foliage
fill home's
fragile morning air
with the hum
of an angel's
cleansing prayer

smoke out my inner critic
release this heaviness
i am too weary to carry
pray your soul will forgive me
as much as it protects me

i await your return
as i charge my crystals
search for your signs
in hand-me-down tarot
call for you in dreams
through sleep spells

you are the one i see
in the meadow when i meditate
you are the one i feel
when i question how to keep living
you are the one i pray will return
each time i burn this white sage

WHEN YOU ASK ME WHY I WRITE POETRY
*after Isabel Rocio, @isabelrocio_*

the intro

prepare for a pause / i am not used to being asked why / why
do i breathe / why do i burrow my feet in the sand / why do i
wait for you day after day

when you ask me why i write poetry / know what you're really
asking for is my soul / i already said no to the devil / but i
imagine you rejecting me will take more of a toll

the truth

i write poetry to touch god / to reach back through soft folds
of time / to reach down my throat / unravel the blood-soaked
knot in my stomach / pull out as much as i can and smear it all
over the page

when you ask me why i write poetry / i'll tell you it's to
remember why i'm here, *why i want to stay alive* / to remember
that i'm here and *i deserve to enjoy this life*

i write poetry to say *this is me* / i write poetry to come home / to
taste electrifying stardust through words that sting the tongue /
to bleed through past lives, to astral project, to meditate / to
transcend

but above all / i write poetry to find / and make love to you.

SPELLCAST

i cross my legs
straighten my back
run my hands
over my thighs

(breathe in, breathe out)

white candles in a circle
an iron cauldron
red sand ablaze
melt the crystalline rock

(breathe in, breathe out)

the ancestors arrive
in a golden daze
they sit and linger
ask about you

(breathe in, breathe out)

"your connection
is through your hands"
they tell me
"trust what
they write"

POCONOS MORNINGS

fresh hyacinth drifts lazily
through the open windows
carried by the same breeze
that kisses my cheek
twirls with the butterflies
glides over the roaring river
and delivers my love to you

Mother Nature likes to play
in the early Sunday hours

as i write word art
in this idyllic forest
i realize our beloved earth
is the real poem

VISION OF THE FUTURE

a home library stuffed with cracked, whispering books, stained with the faint smell of fireplace and jasmine candles; slow sunday mornings with a gentle summer breeze, watching sunlight catch dancing fae fuzzies; a chipped, pink watering can and a garden fat with ripening tomatoes, smelly basil and mint, asparagus peeking through soil, singing sunflowers raising their faces to the sky; a baby's coo breaking the siesta silence, a pitter patter of paw pads on creaking hardwood floors; a healing, growing, glowing earth, where heat wanes for softer days and we treat her pain; wrinkled hands peppered with age spots rocking on the back porch; safe landings on dazzling ancient shores, who open their arms and say, come, learn; leaders who know to keep their hands to themselves; a torch of equality burning bright through history's shadows, lighting the path for our today, our tomorrow; collage journals stacked, stapled and taped with faces of loved ones, pressed flowers, histories of faded jealousies and great belly laughs; salty sea air and gull cries when i open the creaky back door; fresh bread sleeping off its heat on oak cutting boards, blackberry jams and irish butter swollen in grandma's chipped ceramic bowls; your eyes meeting mine over the children chattering, dinner table laden with daily tales and california wine; sinking our feet into earth's sandy cheek as dawn's fruit rises in the sky, leaving footprints behind for my next life.

THE CREATIVE PROCESS

you are a daily practice
a holy habit
the ultimate sacrament

black ink seeps
and stains the paper
my love spell
rolls its eyes back
disappearing in writer's bliss

i make love to you
every day

perfecting the craft
while resurrecting the dead
speaking with gods
birthing storms

i write and
immortalize us both

when the world becomes too much,
too big, too loud, overfilling, overbearing –
i crack open the spine of a well-loved book,
slip into the small spaces between pages;
i fly over neverland, drink wine with achilles,
burrow my hands into earth alongside circe;
i meet santiago and fatima in egypt, i conjure
electricity in my very fingertips, i uncover
a smoking gun with sherlock and annoy
watson with never-ending questions;
i cackle with wicked witches and giggle
over tea with uncle albert and mary;
i find my heart again with the tin man,
command courage with the help of a lion;
i eat gelato in parisian cities i have only
ever seen on maps, i ride dragonback
through kingdoms that only exist on
fiction's breath –

i find home in these spaces,
nursing humanity's sting with characters
who embody the beauty of life in their pages.

when i'm in the clouds, i'm closer to home.
the sky whispers its secrets to me, and suddenly i remember
what it means to fly amongst the angels and soak in dreams.

(a haiku)

a blazing bolt   cracks
an apple down its center
frees eve   from slumber

FREE WRITING

it comes tumbling out of me
all at once
my muses giggle, airborne
fairy wings and glistening trees
wet with morning breath's dew
birds titter and serenade us
as helios yawns and lifts his head
above the horizon, lighting up the world,
morphing the ocean into a pink sheet of glass.

i watch the dolphins tumble amongst
one another, playing in dawn's sweet gaze,
in the sacred silence and hush of early morning.

inhale the fresh tart air,
before everyone wakes,
before the smell of coffee grounds rise
when everything is still and perfect,
we are still and perfect—

i live for those mornings;
find me in the sunrise.

I'M IN LOVE WITH APRIL SHOWERS
(& SHE LOVES ME TOO)

i dip my toes in pastel pools;
i roll cotton candy clouds on my tongue.
i craft sunflower crowns laced in faerie glitter
and stain my lips with ripe blackberry juice.
pink peonies bloom from my irises and
cherry blossoms sleep in my hair –
(i call this mother earth's perfume)

bathing in the dawn's soft birdsong,
my soul feasts on fertile soil and i long
to bury myself amongst hungry seeds.

a spring wind howls and licks my skin
as a thunder shower lazes right on in,
eager to meet the thirsty, bursting buds.
violet rain tumbles from the morning skies,
dripping down to swollen tree branches
where mama green grows and glows
with the equinox's ancient, dusty magic.

i lift my face as lightning dusts the horizon,
ignites our dark earth – spells out my name.

WATER

water

(in the sea)

a rushing explosion of sea spray, and then silence. the kind of quiet only heard under waves and in the womb. water calls to me like a seductive siren. each time i'm submerged in its salty mouth, i am reborn, again and again. the waves rock me like i'm a babe, and i find my soul rests, comforts, and thrives here. my inner voice quells, in awe of its power. perhaps the only time i can silence my demons is when they are reminded of how very small they are. everything seems like it can be solved with salt water and sea breeze.

(in my head)

my mind digs its nails in my throat and holds me under. inner demons cheer, eager to see how long i last before i'm shattering the surface, gasping for air.

depression is no joke.

she lurks in dark violet waters, wishes to hold me close. i'm more terrified of my emotional oceans than the real ones.

let me take on the sharks, as long as they aren't my demons.

my struggles to the surface tire me. i grow numb to everyone around me. i'm a prisoner lost at sea, struggling to smile and not let anyone see. i try to pick up my bloody pieces as they fall out of me. i try to find peace in poetry. if i write my poems in tears, maybe they'll be of use at least. maybe i'll find the way out of the depths through my muses' messages on the pages, maybe through my honesty these waves will part like they did for moses.

here is a snapshot of my sad sea, where finding relief isn't easy. where the pain never becomes pretty.

AURORA'S HOUR

i watch angels extinguish stars across
the night's velvet veil, one by one by one,
blowing out each sleepy, celestial candle
and i wait.

i wait until dawn bleeds
through heaven's ethereal canvas,
stains it a bloody red orange,
then fragile, baby pink.

i search for answers
on the cusp of earth's cheek,
as mellow morning radiance
greets my waking eyes.
and i wonder if light
can flood my emptiness inside,
bring peace to my soul
like it does to this quiet sky.

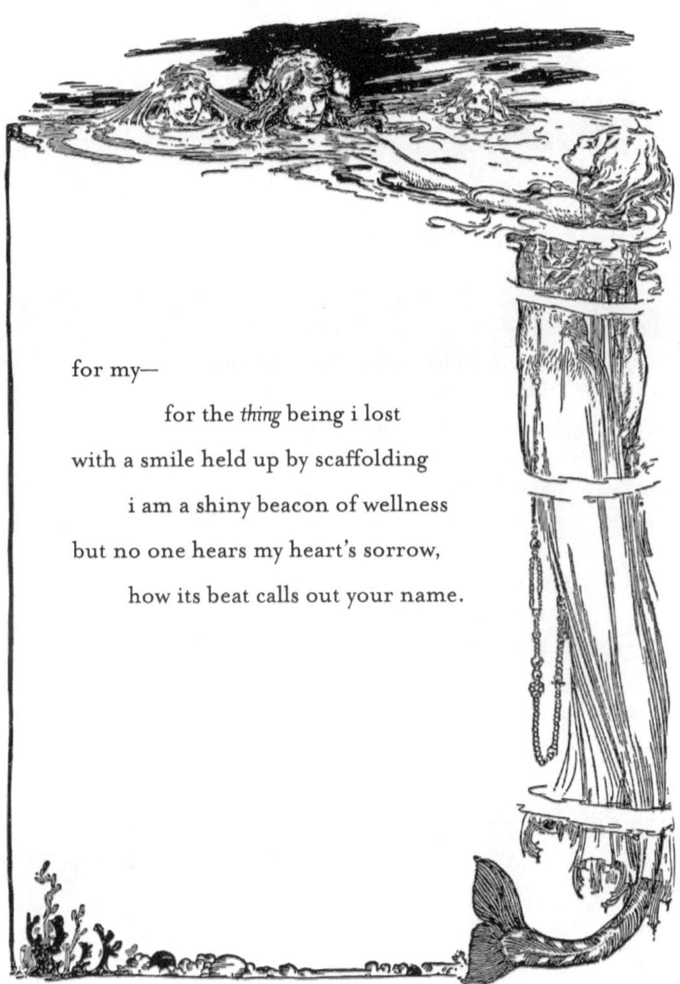

for my—

      for the *thing* being i lost

with a smile held up by scaffolding

      i am a shiny beacon of wellness

but no one hears my heart's sorrow,

      how its beat calls out your name.

i'm a faltering flame, fighting eternal sleep
my devils grin back in chipped glass
rivers rumble, rush, whisper *come with me*
creaky bridges wink as i pass, flirt in the wind

taste the edge of earth
"don't you want to feel glorious
in the end?"

ancient meadows foresee my destiny
prophecies bestowed by our all-knowing sun
heal your inner fire, child, or become undone
i graze my fingers against stars' heat,
           yearning
despair's charred embers fill my palms,
           scorching

i wait for my shadow to fill doorways
i covet my soul in everything i chase
every lover, every joint, every way i breathe
i cling to earth's trees, heaven's gates
desperate to believe
this has all been a mistake

these inner calls for final rest are only
a night terror from which i'll soon wake

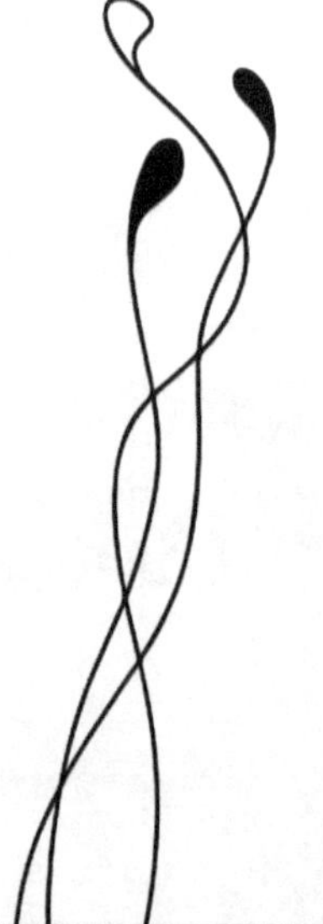

i fill up flimsy papers with sprinkles
of everything left unsaid,
roll them round and round
until a doobie you'd be proud of
rests in my palms like communion.
maybe lighting this will bring
me to salvation.

i pray if i go anywhere, it's to you.

grief daydreams of the one you love
while loss slices skin again
each time the fantasy reaches its end.

but i keep coming back.
knocking on memory's door,
begging for one more look.

i'll bleed out on loss's blade
if it means i die seeing your face.

the world burns
        —i drink
blood slip slopes through stifled streets
my belief that our world is loving, not obscene
finds itself in a rancid gutter drain

i crave a quiet i held as a young child
tracing clouds with delicate humming gazes
where celebrations still thrilled me with sugar highs
and home didn't feel so misplaced

now milestones mark time
fleeing through my fingers
i bottle up memories
to nurse them on my deathbed,
to lucid dream (drunkenly)
to taste hope
        – one last time

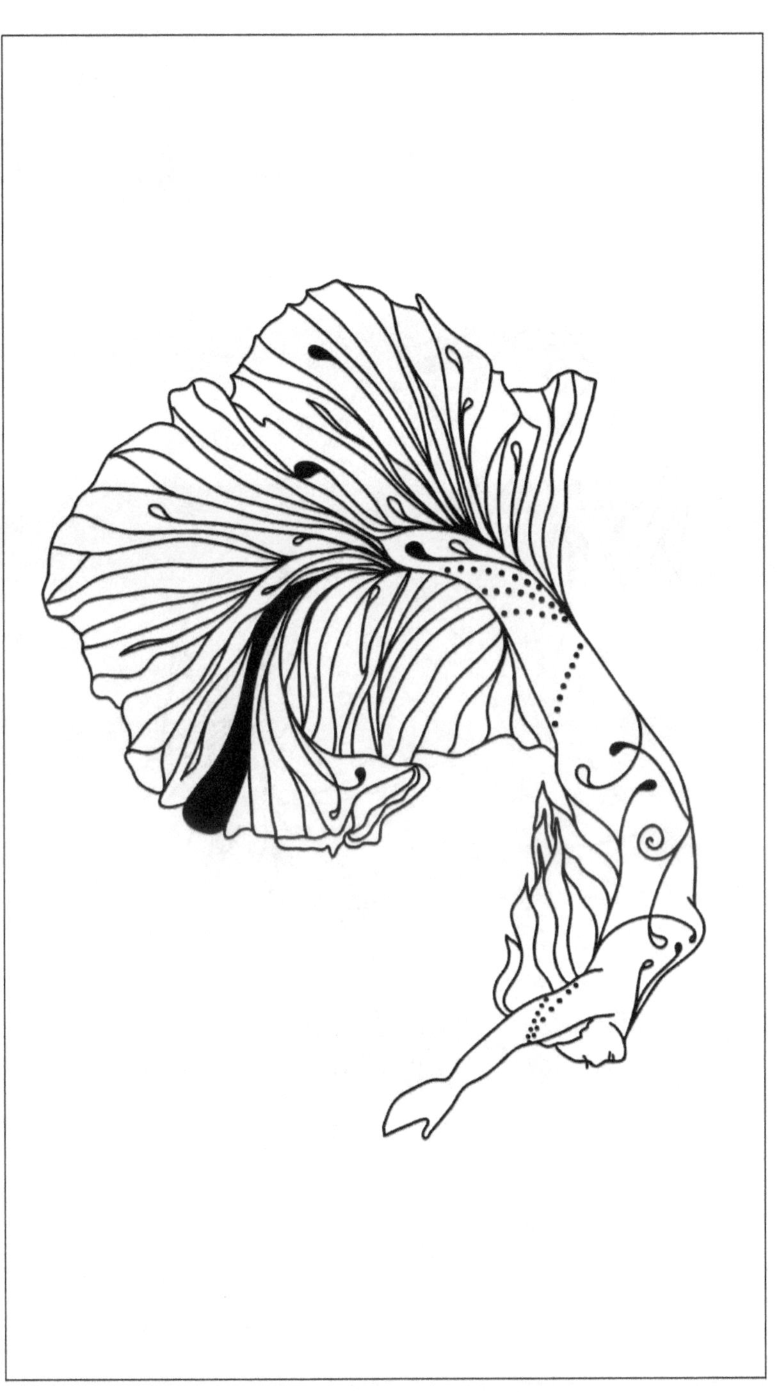

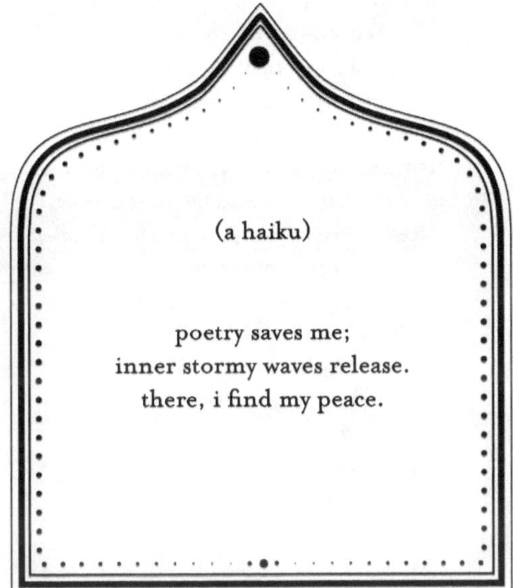
(a haiku)

poetry saves me;
inner stormy waves release.
there, i find my peace.

DISASSOCIATION (AT ITS FINEST)

i'm trying to write the sick out of me
my shoulders are frontlines
a battered soul staring into oblivion
realizing the sky isn't a place
but an endless ongoing space
i melt from my body & stare at the moon
i hover over crowds and let go too soon
free from my mind & prisoner
at the same time
i'm afraid when night falls
i'll dream myself out too far

each time i try to come back
i chant *i'm god's child*
i burrow my feet in the earth
i chant *i'm here, i'm here, i'm here.*

TEXT BACK DAYS LATER

sorry for the late reply
the thing is
i was battling my desire
to die

i don't want to move on
just yet you see
but my inner demon whispers
this is the end of me

LOST SOUL (REWARD: LIFE OF CONTENTMENT)

where do i go
  when i disassociate?

where does my soul slip
   to as my vacant eyes
 grow dispassionate?

does it burrow in ancient rivers?
   trip over asteroids
 yearning for home?
does it drown itself in liquor
   on a sunny day in Rome?

does my soul long to come back?
    does it miss me too?
i need it you see
  for without it
i'm blue

HAPPY NEW YEAR

winter sinks its teeth in me
my skin fractures as my heart seizes
chasing ghosts is what i do most seasons
phantoms of past selves i've shed
surround me whispering
it's not so bad being dead

we lift frothy, foggy glasses
to the new year
as i ponder where
to go from here

in my starless hour
i believed death
would be the best lover
how arrogant
and naive
of me

i cooed half-true
i want yous
to the grim reaper
teetered on the edge
of consent and
before i could summon
my dark angel

he knocked on my door
pressed his lips to mine
murmured—*are you sure?*

we stood at the edge
of the universe
as blood dripped down my legs
desire gifted to me
in the wrappings of
a curse

heaviness settles softly
a sticky fog polluting pores
with filthy residue labeled
anxiety and *worthless*

suffocating my inner light
encouraging the darkness
to yawn and stretch
take a seat in my blood

smirk at my distress
the ever returning
unwelcome guest—

the monster is home, honey

cackles echo in my ears
and before i stand a chance
i fall through the fog and

my eyes bleed into
a pearly white trance.

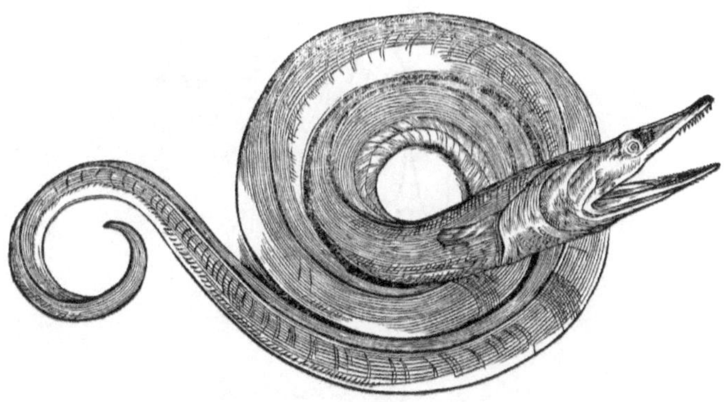

black ink pours from my eyes
spirits rise one last time
this is the language of grievers
desperate for holy water
to heal this self-hate fever

my body emits
silent screams
as anxiety taunts me
with terror dreams
of licking my blood
and ink off faith's floors

i am raw
like a newborn chick
splitting through the shell
that fostered my growth

i am raw
like an open wound
the slick, dark blood
dripping down my neck

i am raw
like an earthborn soul
fresh from the goddess's womb
feeling earth's ancient dirt
beneath my feet for the first time
and realizing
this ache in my chest
is humanity

GRIEF

devastation arrives like a tidal wave
and knocks me off my feet

i'm caught in an
undercurrent of loss
a riptide of mourning
a stunning defeat

beneath these tears
i gasp for breath
and beg for release

witnessing my struggle
to the saltwatery surface
helios reaches out and weeps

"this sea of pain you're drowning in,
this bleeding grief—
why, it is nothing but love, my darling,
bittersweet."

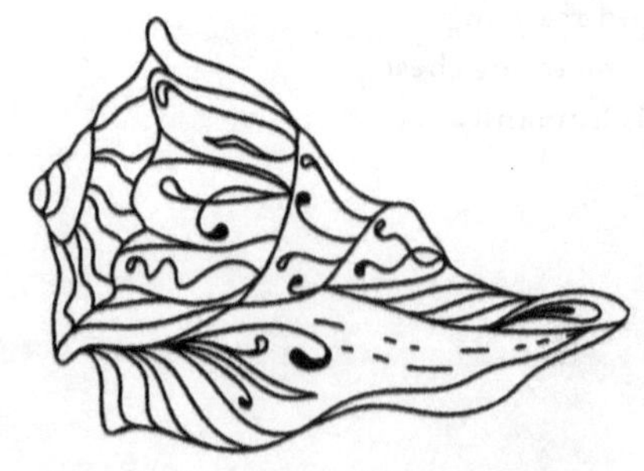

6AM & GLOOMY

mornings like these
i avoid the mirror,
i avoid the page,
like fear
steers clear
of rage.

writing about
the darkness
means facing
the wickedness,
and acknowledging
my brittleness.
how can i let myself,
my words,
bleed with distress?
though truthfully,
it's what i know best—
this beast inside of me,
always shackled to my chest.

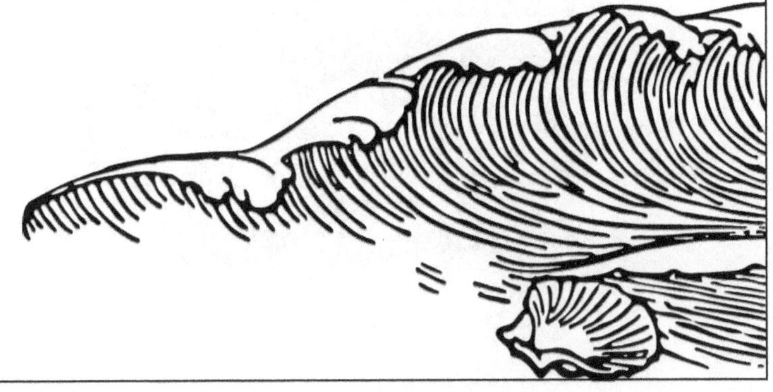

VULNERABILITY

my claws slice into my bare flesh
and peel open my chest
to show you who i really am

this nakedness is more terrifying to me
than the monsters in the shadows
because you could oh so easily
wrap your fingers
around my pulsing heart
and be the end of me

ON HARD DAYS THE BIRDS HELP

a freckled mourning dove lands on my window's lower lip,
coos the dawn's dewy news in her delicate tune.
she carries a note from the yellow yolk rising over earth's hip,
reminding me — soft, then searing —
                          you are — alive, you are — alive.

this is a body, not a rat race. this is a body, not a dollar sign.
this is your body, not an identity.

my heart beats like a blinking, vacant motel sign.
i ask the dove to find my soul.
if she does, how far can she carry it?
is it as heavy as this emptiness?
maybe she could take me across the Appalachians,
maybe we could find our way to La Jolla's shores.
my tongue craves the taste of the wind,
my skin itches to run my fingers through clouds.
i ache to remember that i am a creature of earth like her.

i inhale sunshine, watch my exhale stir its beams.
the dove stays. she eyes me, coos again.
you are — alive.

i am tired of the ache
for all it offers
is a slight beg
with a touch of grief
topped in mourning

i am the castaway
washed upon the shore
an alien to this world
a witch among mortals
a holy, wanderlust soul
light-years from home

MY JUNK DRAWER IS FULL, TELL ME WHERE TO PUT MY PAIN

i try to stuff it between my ribs, the same ones they claim adam
made me from. but this fragile cage of bones shrieks in protest,
recognizing the scent of men's violence,
far too familiar to our origin.

people i know pick up their pain in great globs and lob them at
everyone's faces, pour pain into their loved ones' laps.

(hurt people - hurt - people)

i bring mine to the backyard, dig a grave beneath the lemon tree
and attempt to bury it next to my sins. archeologists will
stumble across my hidings 1,000 years from now and say

see how they buried everything?
see how they gave back to earth?

i walk like a beggar in the street with bloody feet, trying to pawn
off my aching and hoping to obtain something to sustain me

only when i put pen to page does the anguish begin to fade

anxiety builds like lava beneath mother earth's cracked, tectonic
plates. i tremble the way i do when i'm with you, but instead of
anticipating the sun's lazy rise, a mass of crows beat their wings
in my chest, warning me danger is near and my legs quake and
my breath catches. even when the hyenas are kept at bay and the
weather sighs into a quiet calm, all is well, i am tight with stress,
looking for the next hunter to ascend above the rolling hills,
eager to strike me down. lightning bugs whisper that i can rest
tonight; they will guard me through the sun's slumber, but my
thumping heart jolts awake like a sudden summer storm's strike
of lightning at 3am, convinced if i look in the mirror
i will see streaks of wet scarlet blood across my face.

(i am safe)

my body is a moon
births waves
in a steaming bathtub

(i am safe now)

my rust-stained skin
paints traces
of loss in bubbles

(i am safe)

FIRE

fire

i have moons for eyes yet the sun brews beneath my collarbone.

i taste flames, let them flicker across my tongue like a dull, aching hangover. i evoke fire with my fingertips, let the blaze dance in my hands.

once i burned bright, then out, like a dying star. again and again, i grew flowers, only to watch them lie limp in my arms. dried out in a loveless drought. burnt from a lust fire.

i craved fire more than the high of his hand on my thigh. i liked watching myself smolder, crack open, see pain ooze out.

i became so skilled at playing with flames, i'd balance out the perfect amount of high and fall. other days, i got right to burning. i'd stack wood and pine and debate the oils i'd wear to the altar. then i'd summon tornados, hurricanes, floods, as if i was calling on the end of time—

cold asphalt stung my cheek. bleary-eyed, i blinked through black smoke. ash coated me like a protective blanket, like god's arms. i heard faint whispers but there was no one in the room other than the wind. i lifted my head in rebirth, walked out of the fire's womb. i learned to breathe again, walk again, talk again, eventually even think about you.

afterwards, i dreamt i was rosemary and fire bled down my legs. it reminded me of the bathroom floor; it reminded me of the brown waiting room. memories skyrocket before my eyes like comets before impact. i drop them one by one in the grass.

like a weathered, fertile crater, like a deceased volcano's mouth, my phoenix soul illuminates in ashy soil. grows. glows.

oh, to love such a man—

with emotions running
like deep, starry rivers
right beneath the surface
of your stoic flesh.

an ancient soul dipped
and adorned in gold,
with the power of a god
brewing beneath your crown.

your fingers trail my naked back
as if my life story is laid out in braille
and you are unraveling every secret
i've woven into my skin since birth

MIRAGE

my mouth is full of oranges, fat with juice
i'm blissful in the sun's mellow afternoon
through summer's stillness, i hear your heart
a sweet siren symphony, your finest art

i love, i love, i love
        i love you.

you promised me the sea
devotion   no one can take from me
cicadas hum their conjuring
July, in earthy heat, sheds   shimmer
i blink twice
      (is it you?)
sunburn litters my skin with love bites

DAVID

my knees kiss marble feet
i beg, pleading my love to speak
if only i had fairy dust
maybe i could make him breathe
a twitch of the mouth
a smile breaking free
lover, let's get lost in serendipity
but statues do not budge, do not agree
instead he stares ahead patiently
as if there's nothing to care for in sight
with or without me, immobility is
home, where he feels right
i could lie dying before him
and i wouldn't be worth the fight

what do you call love
which lacks the ability to ignite?

our shadows kiss in golden hour glow
outlines of our soul becoming whole
i think this is how i'll remember you most
an aura bursting in orangey gold
it's only fitting your energy gleams eternally
blinding us both

you are light

you are love

you are sunshine

from above

THE TRUTH ABOUT US

you and i were
a smoking ship on a fool's errand;
a sparking, ricocheting rocket;
we were rubbing, serrated fault lines;
feisty, misfiring synapses;

we were wounded children;
the cherry stem you tie on your tongue;
we were ravenous, greedy pirates;
and we were thick as thieves –

each other's favorite rum and disease.
you were adam in this story, i was eve;
i tasted possibility,

    (fled)

unearthed the woman
i was meant to be

if you mean it
ink it in my skin
i want to carry this moment
with me til the very end

a living tomb engraved
in scarlet letters
i'll wear your devotions
on me like scripture

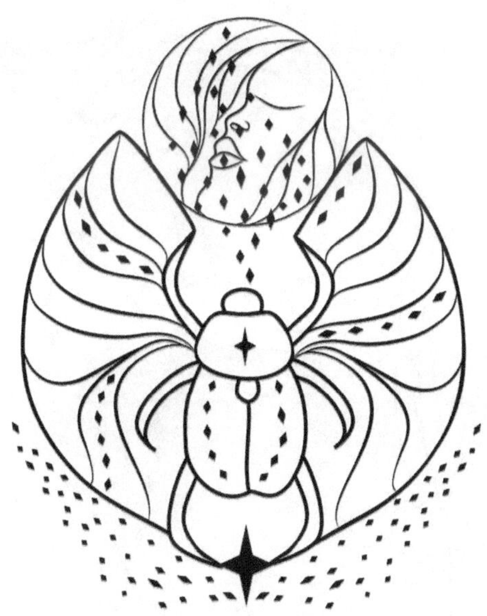

I AM ONE WHO LOVED NOT WISELY BUT TOO WELL

until my soul burned through the sheets that mummified our
sleeping bodies, until desperation ran in hot tears down my face,
until i breathed air for you instead of me.
it's like i let out a siren call for broken inner children to come
running while mine played hide and seek. fed a wound so pure it
dripped gold by the end. drank my ignorance from a chalice and
became drunk off it.
i am one who loved not wisely but too well.
until emptiness lurked in my breath, until my stomach lay
barren, until i realized i was my only salvation.

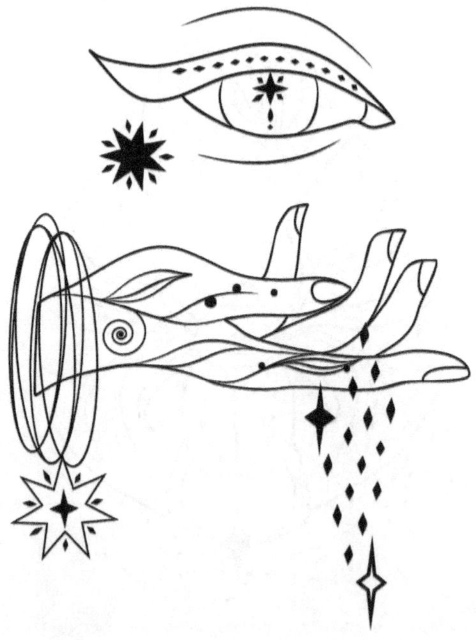

TITLE FROM SHAKESPEARE'S "OTHELLO"

i love how your presence brings me peace
safety is your arms lulling me to sleep
home is finding you again in my dreams

DEPORTACIÓN

it was quiet when you left—
the sky opened and wept with me
as the same wind that stroked my jawline
carried you to safety 3,000 miles away

it was quiet when you left—
the only presence i craved was yours,
ravenous, in a society dedicated to starving
its people

it was quiet when you left—
the stars stilled and prayed with me
as mother moon hugged us both

candlelight
          flickers
                    like fairy wings
while
     rain
          knocks
                    on the windowpane

film credits
          race
                    down
                         the silent screen

the same way
          your tongue
                    does on me

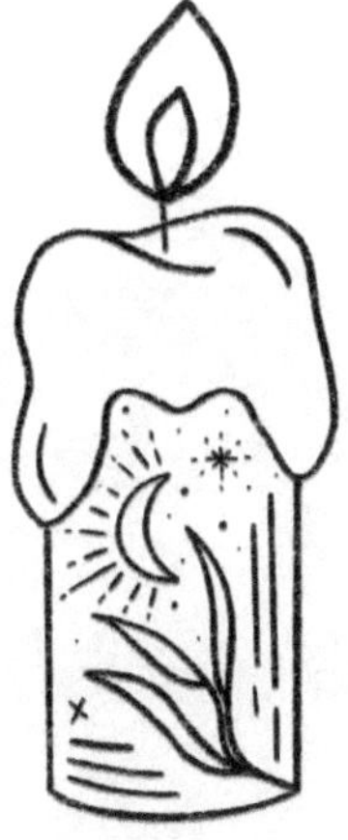

CASANOVA (OR PERHAPS, NARCISSUS)

lips pressed against mine, staining them poppy red. under your
spell, all i dreamt of was your scent. call me a love-hungry
vampire, but you were the emotional one. your true nature hid
behind decadent lies you spun. tying me tight in your sugary
poisonous webs, i prayed for the day you and i would wed.
but your kisses left toxic residue on my cheeks, charred bits of
sweet words ruddied with deceit. two steps ahead of me, face in
the shadows, i reached for you only to grasp sorrow.

you planted sweet, poisonous weeds of doubt.
wiry roots dug through brain matter and insecurity bled from
my mouth. i'm the one you loved, but i was crazy. i'm the one
you loved, but this was too much, maybe. when i asked who she
was, you asked how i could ever think you'd betray me.

when i saw you walk down the aisle thirteen months later,
i thought, of course, who else would it be?

like spotting
the old flame
you never stopped
loving
the sun blushes
when she stumbles
across the moon
mid-rise

YOU ASK ME ABOUT MY FIRST LOVE
after Shannon Stephan, @writtenbyshannon

and i'm whispering *te quiero mucho* as dawn's light pools through
crooked curtains, anointing your dreaming face; i'm in lecture,
blushing at your love songs and doodles scribbled on scraps
tucked throughout my english lit notebooks; we're eating with
Mama as she calls me *favorite daughter* over the gallo pinto and
you beam at me like the sun; i'm in coney island—it's balmy
mid-july as we rip into smoked fish chased with russian beer—
grimy, gritty brooklyn sand between our toes; i'm in a white
windowless courtroom as *marriage is your only option* drops on our
eighteen- and twenty-year-old laps; we're walking in dead winter
with wind as cold as your shoulder, searching for a pawn shop
that'll buy the gold ring; it's 2am after another house party,
dubstep and drunks muffling our sloppy, misfired profanities;
we're sinking in silence on a rusty park bench, until finally, a
question erupts: *is this it?*; a miami area code is calling and when
i answer, you tell me there's seven minutes before your last flight
out of america; we're whispering *this isn't goodbye but—*

g o o d b y e, tears and apologies lodging in our throats,
everything left unsaid drowning us both.

like a bedraggled sailor
        finding a siren lost at sea
you, my beloved, c o m m a n d
        all of me

i lick the rum from your lips
stand at attention(!)
        when you demand it

i ask the sky
        how broken did i have to be?
for you to prey upon me
gifted trauma dumps
followed by love bombs' glee

i love you but the truth is
        you've only been poisoning me

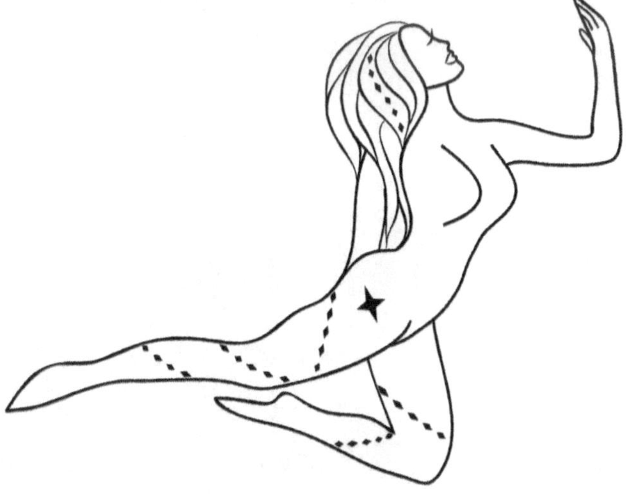

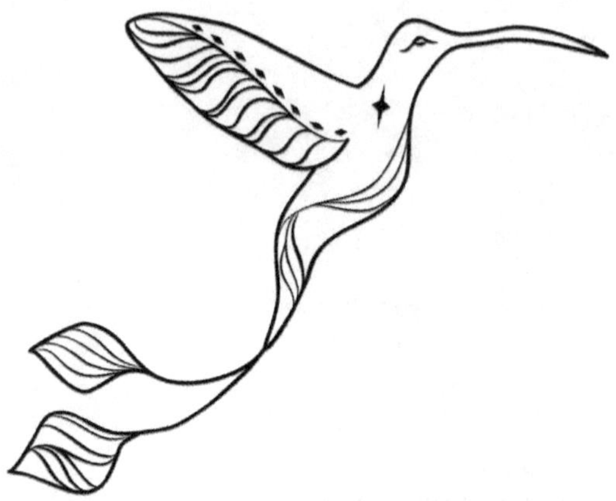

zen connection grounds us together
readying our roots for coming centuries
a predestined union my inner eye failed to prophesize
nirvana is only revealed when you're ready
dare i thank god too soon; dare we enjoy this?
you and me—*foreva eva, foreva eva*—
never letting love be anything but bliss.

I AM SORRY I AM NOT HER

but you will never forget me—i am the bitter tart lemon
slipping and stinging your wounded mouth; i am the bridge and
outro of *come thru* gripping you by the neck and whispering my
name in your ear (no matter what company you're in, no matter
where you are, your heart double thuds);

i am in the background of a mad men episode, the lonely extra
smoking a joint with a glass of dark whiskey in hand;
i am the slight breeze on a miami evening whispering
be free, be free, be free;
i am the shot burn in the back of your throat at the tiki bar;
i am the number you swear you'll never need
but its home is buried in your notes app;

i am sorry i am not her—
but you will try to forgive me for it.
what is the opposite of a soulmate?
if a soulmate is the protagonist in this story,
what does that make you?
i am sorry i am not her—

i am the *apology* that was finally uttered, *better late than never, right?*
i am all of your forgotten fantasies and broken promises;
i am the dusty skeleton in the closet; i am every blonde you see;
your secret succubus, haunting dreams you never speak of;
i am the door that never quite closes;
i am sorry i am not her
(i'm just the one you wonder about).

I AM SORRY I AM NOT HER (PART II)

i'm sorry i'm not the one you want
i'm the bitter tart fruit that
stings your tongue
slices into your memory
and imbeds myself
in brain pathways
so each way you turn
there i am—

i'm the split-second daydream
the *i wonder where she is now*
i'm the song you randomly shuffle
once a year
that takes you back
to 2013
i'm the late-night texts and
hotel room haunts
the canary yellow of sunflowers
and lemon drops
i'm the one you sat with
in that waiting room and
i'm the breeze of a miami night

but most importantly
i'm not her
and for that
i thank god

during the dark years, when a veil shielded my
eyes from myself, i reached for you through
orion's cosmic dust to clasp hands, brush bod-
ies – drown in you, like a greedy drunk making
love to the bottle.

i never craved a crown or a throne besides yours.
i thirsted for the somersaults in my stomach, my
heart's loud hum as our eyes held each other's –
i yearned for the click of your front door
opening, your grin waiting behind it. i could
watch you walk towards me forever – play it back
– rewind it; i worshipped our bond, believed
we were timeless.

so we tiptoed, toppled, over the high's taut
tightrope. if i hit the sweet spot just right, no
ambrosia was as tantalizing as the anticipation
of you. will you love me? will you choose me?

my drug of choice was the possibility,
not the answer.
my drug of choice was you contemplating,
not you choosing.

we both know how it ended. how we drank each
other's toxins until we were gaunt in the face.
until, like any other drug, we began to consume
too much, destroying not only ourselves, but
our beloveds; until collateral damage piled up
so high neither of us could deny it.

a cleansing, a withdrawal,
a goodbye *for good this time* –
these were all cures necessary for survival.

UNION, NEW JERSEY

my phone lights up
i hate sleeping alone
only two exits down 78
there's almost no excuse
to say no to you

two drinks in but i tell myself
i can manage, we got this
arrogance grabs my keys
as lust follows giddy out the door

the driver is fear masked
by adrenaline, lust whines
from the backseat
are we there yet

you're waiting by the door
when the engine cuts
you smile at lust
as i climb the steps

but self-destruction
is the one who greets you

DON'T THINK YOU'RE SPECIAL

you inspire good art
but once i immortalize you in words
i seal the envelope with a kiss
and my heart is set free

I AM THE LOVER IN YOUR DREAMS

my love for you strums my vocal chords
and discolors my lips until they look like
they've been kissed by a sugary snowstorm
of my sickly-sweet words—
words i never thought i'd be saying in this lifetime,
a love i thought i had forfeited until my next
reincarnation, *i swore i missed you this round—*

take a slice of my madness / destiny's worn watch
wheezes as it climbs past midnight /
i don't know how much time we have

lunacy tastes of key lime drizzled in ocean tears;
i slip my tongue in your mouth to savor it, too;
when you close your eyes / know i'm with you
when you wake tomorrow / know i'll be missing you.

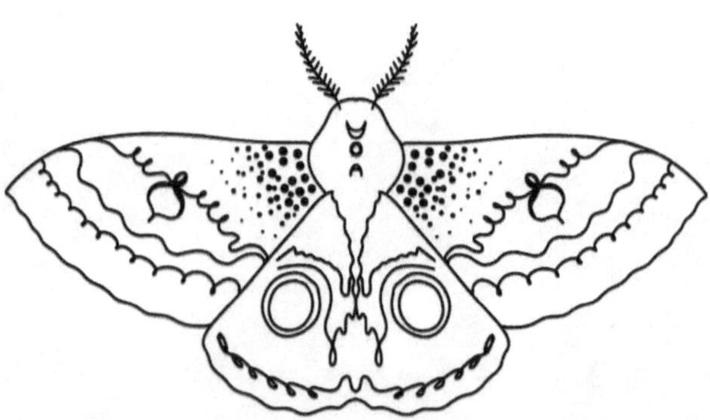

ARIES

a sparkler soul
captivating, crackling,
the type to shock like
an unexpected kiss;
the out-of-the-blue,
sugary, tart, *i want you too—*

swallow me whole
let me trace the insides
of your being and leave
a trail of butterflies
in my wake

listen to their teasing
the answers to the riddles
will always bring you
back to me

CONJURING

the sky swells with my rage
i call upon the winds to
send a twister and destroy us

i don't know how else to
pull this love out of my chest

let the seas rise
at my command
sweep through the streets
drown the damage we've done
soak the bondage of our lies
until they've rotted away
like our love

SUNDAY AT THE BEACH

you emerge from the sea
with salt crystals and water weeping
down your body and when the sunlight hits just right
it looks as though lava is dripping down your skin
a man of the elements, a man of the gods
walking towards me as if i am the only thing
left on earth, as if i am the only thing that will
bring him salvation. *i am your king,* he says to me
and i smirk because i have never been a woman
in want of a king and you roar,
launch your wet body at mine. we collide like
two meteors desperate to merge; perhaps we
have done this before, perhaps we have done
this in every lifetime and when you lift your gaze
to meet mine, our mouths open wide
with laughter, i say
i love you
i fucking love you

truth is, i miss you
with your resting bitch face
that cracks into the most beautiful smile
when i say something that's impressed you

i miss the rants, the sleepy rambles,
the defiance of dreamers free to be
themselves in each other's presence
because *you get me*
you just get me

you get me under the sheets
i tell you *this is who i am*
and when the delirium fades
we wonder how much time has
passed in our sacred oasis

but as the moon travels
i realize my hands
don't know you anymore
and all i can do is pray
you're brought back to me

but until the stars fall
i am your stranger

pink skies,
the sun's rise.

(this awe inside.)

that's how i feel
when i look in your eyes.

will you miss me when i'm gone?
you always said *i am so lucky*
my energy, my body
a gift you stumbled upon
by sheer dumb luck

but i disagree
this is no serendipity
because meeting a soul like you
can only be divine intervention

i know you
i've walked with you
once upon a dream
or however it goes

all i know
is your soul feels like home
and we both have the gift
of seeing angels walk amongst us

like that time you told me
you saw god in the mountains
and i didn't have the heart to tell you
i always see god in your eyes

my mouth split open
like a branch hit by lightning
and my bony white fingers
stepped over my sap-filled tongue
and crept down my throat
looking for my soul's home

my heart volunteered itself
as it always will for you
with a nod and hushed goodbyes
ready to relinquish the crown
if it meant sparing pain in your eyes

CURSIVE PIROUETTES

your hand lies
between my thighs
and you ask me
if i love you
only you
who do you love
your fingers slip
up
down
round and
round
i gasp as you spell out your name
in pretty
cursive
pirouettes

as i lie upon your chest,
your heart purrs bewitching lullabies
and whispers sweet stories in my ear.

the curtains of my eyes fall,
as your love rocks me to sleep.

maybe in another lifetime
i will turn my head to the left
to greet your grin, before your eyes
turn back to the open road.

maybe in another lifetime,
breakfast will always mean coffee
and a kiss from you.

maybe in another lifetime
love will mean our home,
and distance never more than
a few feet away.

MAYBE IN ANOTHER LIFETIME (PART II)

maybe in another lifetime,
i will plant my bare feet to the soil,
allow spindly and wiry, vast and burly roots
to erupt from my heels and burrow deep
into earth's womb.

maybe in another lifetime,
i will sit on a worn rocking chair out back
as thunder rolls through with rage,
our baby breathing in and out, in and out,
tiny eyes shut against electricity's blade,
illuminating our life for precious seconds.

maybe in another lifetime,
we will grow ripe in age, wiser, quieter—at peace,
with red poppies and a warbler's song
bringing us back to life, your hand in mine,
the damp dirt beneath us, finally enough,
sown in our home.

EARTH

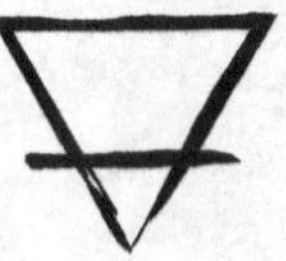

earth

grounding and rebirth.

the quiet after the storm.

i stood alone in my apartment, my first home, all on my own. i lit candles and saged, invited the ancestors in. white cotton curtains trailed their fingers against my hardwood floors. eucalyptus mated with steam and my bathroom became a spa.

moment by moment, breath by breath, barefoot to floor. i picked up parts of myself i'd dropped without realizing. my love for writing. my compassion. my patience. my own self-value, stripped bare and left behind before the fall. i washed them in my tub and cleansed their energy with quartz winking in twilight. i sat on the floor and held my own gaze in the mirror, wondering how we got here. listening to my eyes tell me their story.

how they begged for me to listen.

how every disaster was fueled by their suffering. oh, how they were just trying to get my attention.

i met with my younger self in meditation. we walked together through the highlands back in Scotland and wrote together on the banks of the Thames. we hiked up ancient volcanos which purred beneath our feet. we listened to god on the same field our ancestors erected temples.

the palms of my feet kissed earth and grew roots. i remembered i can withstand the tsunamis and fires as long as i breathe and feel the ground beneath my being.

i began to see my soul like an ancient tree, weaving its growth through layers of this celestial body. tinge my tree's rings with cosmic mist and healing.

at some point along the way
i lost my soul
i buried her
mistaking her darkness
for weakness
forgetting the goddess in me
is me.

an angel eavesdrops on my springtide dreams
plants yellow daisies in the soil of my soul
i shedded grief like a second skin all winter
in ostara's first light, i conjure joy to grow

PLEASE DON'T MAKE THIS POEM ABOUT YOU

because it's not. it's about the places and spaces
i've been—even if that includes your lips,
your first home's couch, your mother's kitchen—

old lovers decorate my skin in scars
       what caused you and what broke you
and how did you mend?

anyone i've ever loved feels like
a broken bone's deep ache in the rain
no longer bolts of lightning to the heart
no longer craters i'm desperate to fill
but rich fertile earth and fragrant forests
begging me to look within

my anger burned bright along trauma's creases
until nothing was left but smoking ashes
it rained and rained until i surrendered to my pain
only then could i tame the beasts inside of me

but what one calls *ashes*
         i call stardust
forever evolving
     forever beating
          forever buzzing

so you could say in the arms of a star i was born
and when i woke i heard god in my head

please don't make this poem about you

because it's not. it's about the places and spaces
i've been—and once i found healing within,
i thanked my lovers for the treasure map
dotted in lessons to who i've become

because i learned to love my soul
and embracing myself
     is where rebirth begins

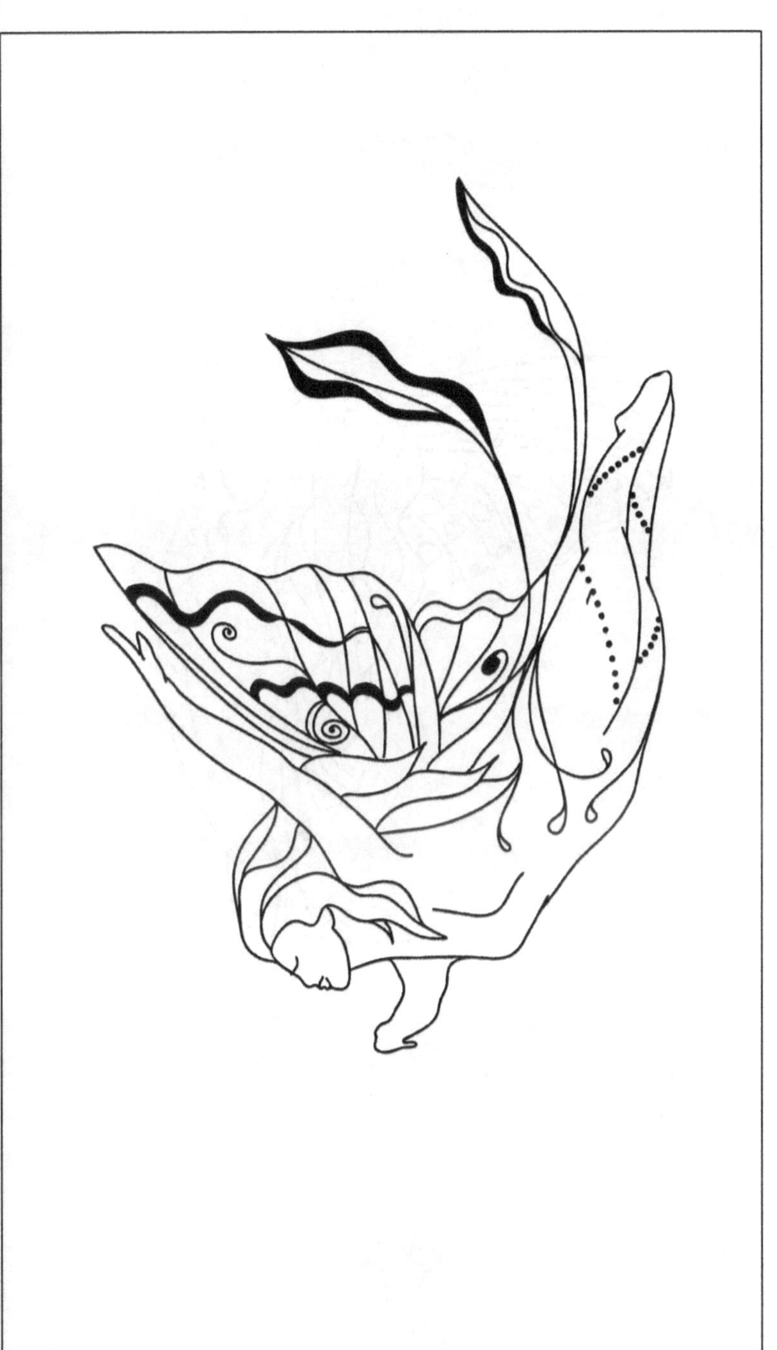

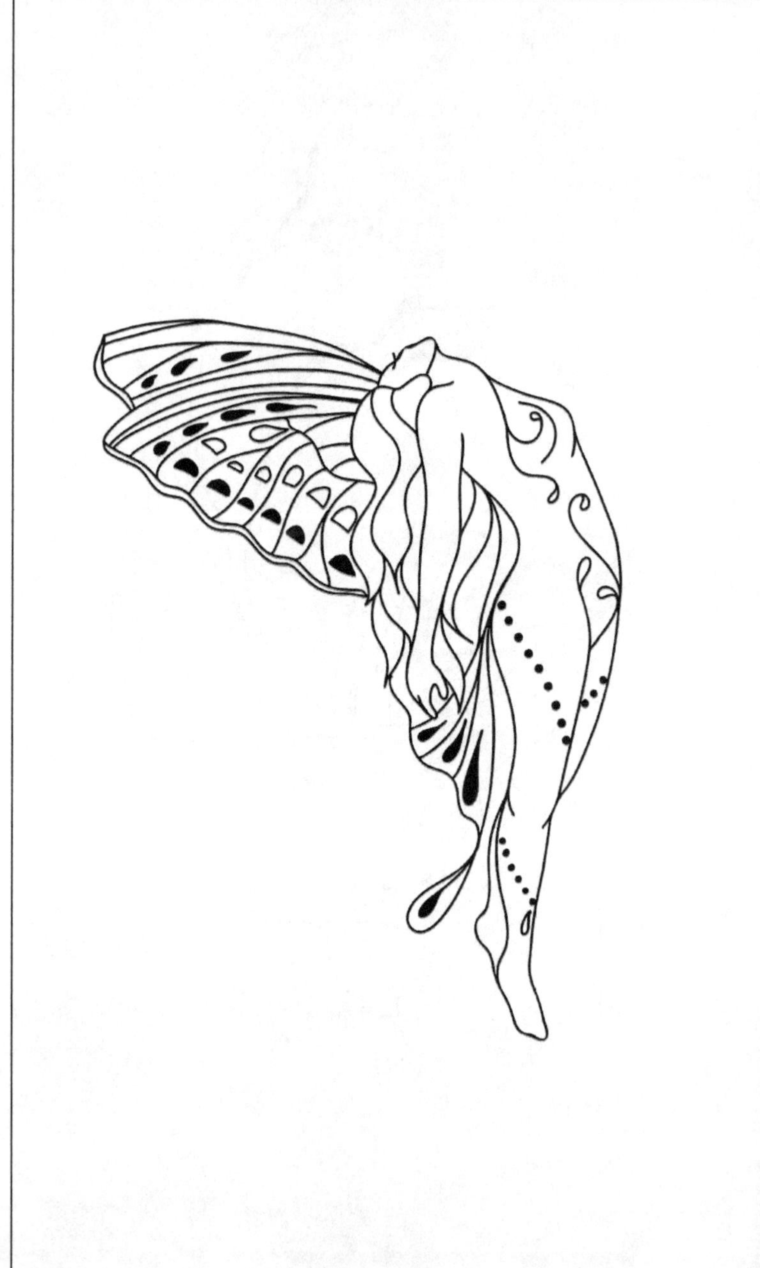

EVERYONE BRAVE IS FORGIVEN

i take my insides out and polish them
     everything starts as a seed
why plant these demons willingly
     they're expensive to feed

a goddess awakens within me
     i am my own true love's kiss
she demands we dance and be brave
     don't fall back into the abyss

grasp the hands of your younger self
     it's okay, i love you, be brave
how else could this end?
     to find peace, i forgave.

TEMPORARY HIGHS
inspired by snoh aalegra

my right foot pushing off a cliff's rocky face, tasting infinity's sting / plunging, plunging, plunging down into mother ocean's cool kiss / a trail of pixie dust and a club's throbbing bass / silky laguna water carrying me along its surface, as volcanos rumble sleepily / touching wet clouds from a mountain's peak / locking eyes with a newborn angel, sharing a smile / taking a hit and melting, melting, melting / music waves caressing my skin and crooning in my ear / a book's climax / feet pounding against earth's cheek / a sunrise's good morning wink / a loved one's joyous cackle / your breath tickling my neck / falling in love with the art you make / feeling god in everything you create

ALL MY FRIENDS ARE HAVING BABIES AND I JUST WANT TO GET DRUNK IN ROME

please, have all the babies.

let me kiss tiny foreheads and smell from the fountain of youth. they are my coven—for you are, too.

and, truthfully, i danced with the idea of staring into the eyes of a freshly earthbound soul birthed from my flesh.

but right now all i want to do is get drunk in rome. to roll freshly squeezed grapes along my tongue and let the sun leave butterfly kisses against my cheeks, staining them baby pink. to feel laughter tickle its way up my spine, my best friend's giggle meeting mine in harmony. i want to walk around museums in complete silence, feel our ancestors' holiness twirl around me— their whispers a gentle breeze fluttering my skirt. lie on white, crisp sheets with my lover as wind cools our bodies. delve deeper into my own layers.

for i am the sea and there is so much of me.

cookie cutter homes seem ten, twenty years away and yet 1992 slips farther and farther out of sight. and earth continues to do the jig around the sun, thirty times for me, at least, and society grabs my shoulders—pressing down, down, down.

women hand me ticking clocks daily now. in their homes as i eat at their kitchen tables, while i lean against cold countertops booking doctor appointments, at the nail salon as i ask for white polish. i want to thrust their little time bombs back into their sweaty palms. flash a tight smile, thank them, then slap! them across the face. not to cause them harm but to wake them up from this demanding dream.

wake up, wake up, wake up.

i look at the men in my life and their homes breathe sleepily and silently while mine grows louder, ticking like a never-ending cicada summer. hope lives in their homes while she is buried alive in mine.

the world is your oyster and you can be anything you want to be seem like silly fairytales and promises of Father Christmas—fables told to us as children to dull the ache of society's expectations.

breed, breed, breed before your expiration date arrives; see it there, tatted just beneath your loose lock of hair. and i thank our ancestors for removing the gun to our heads but society hides it better now. no need for a gun when a slow poisoning will work just fine.

i want mimosas in rome. to feel sun's life pour into my pores.

i want to breathe without the countdown.

i swallow each clock one by one
    and let them detonate inside me.

CHILD OF EARTH

i speak the language of blossoms,
of rainstorms, of cheeky sun;
every dawn my soul hums in greeting
and wind wraps me in reverent hugs.
i am a child of soil and moon,
the child of delicate birdsong.
my naked feet greet grass
giving thanks to earth
the trees welcome me home
and offer their ripest fruit;
i buzz with life and wonder
how humanity drifted
so far from its roots.

MEDITATIVE SPACES

lime green grass, one of nature's treasured rugs. in the middle of a laguna, on a weathered-down dock, with earth's tectonic plates rumbling beneath me. silence surrounded by sleeping blankets of cloud-white snow. a sanctuary, my first apartment's living room littered with protective crystals, enchanting candles and sunrise captured in a lamp. mother ocean's waves, rocking. my cat purring in my lap. in a bubble bathtub with billie singing. a silent smoke cyph with people i love who do not demand conversation for comfort. dawn, water, birds—calling.

i walk with god each time.

i create worlds within me
drop in for visits during meditation
step into white lights,
visit vast universes imbedded in me

since time was a newborn
ancient stardust simmers in my veins
here, my void dims
for everything i seek is within

i am the essence of home

RITUALS

i collect water to bathe in the moonlight;
i wash out my soul to start anew—
a reincarnation, a baptism, a cleansing.
a pinch of forgiveness blended with acceptance
creates a pearly residue on my skin.
i glow, charged by celestials.
i thank my former self for getting me here
while i plant her in my garden.
healed seedlings birth glorious foliage.

flurries flutter like fairies
past my window announcing the arrival
of the winter solstice, and magic pours
from my fingertips as the muses rejoice.
i feel it in my bones, in my blood,
the ancient pull to slumber, to hibernate,
to recharge.
the call for rest.
the call for rebirth.

I COULD DO THIS FOR THE REST OF MY LIFE

love you
love me
feel peace when greeting the blue sea
fall deep into lines of weeping, streaming poetry
catnaps on woven, lakeside hammocks
christmas eve in matching pajamas
bathe in bubbles reeking of jasmine
bask in awe under the moon
feel your laugh swell my heart
like a big bright balloon
fall into my mom's protective hug
make a wish on summer's first lightning bug
watch thick theater curtains open
bathed in soft light
pour my soul into everything i write

between storm breaks, we tremble.
in the aftermath, we weep.
in solitude, we listen.

i refuse to let this chaos take my peace.

sink inwards; go deep.
breathe in, then out; release.
divinity cannot be taken from you.
it's your birthright, what you seek.

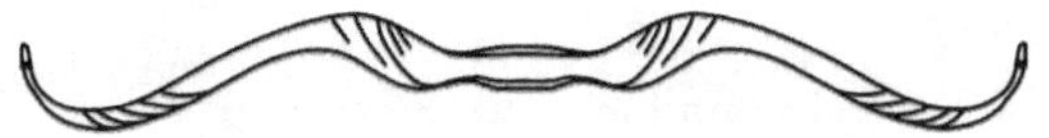

DOUBT

maybe meaning is in
these echoes i pour from my pen
maybe solace lies in
we may never know how
or why or even when

maybe the voice i trust
most is my own; maybe
the angel who whispers

bathe your frigid pain
in scorching forgiveness

is me finding my way home.

A WOMAN'S FIRST MISTAKE
IS PUTTING HERSELF SECOND

i admit i'm a little messed up
(this skin you see me wearing isn't mine)
consider this my poetic confession
(i must weed out the demons in my coffin before i sleep)

when you left i bit into a cursed apple for the first time
(if you pray for emptiness, death will kiss you)
carried your rejection like a scarlet letter
(ladies, never confuse a man for a god)
destroyed the woman i was to rebuild
(burning bridges can inflame the entire village)

you moved on but somehow i was dead
(they call it *ghosting* but it's you they murder in the story)
i mourned a narcissist before morphing into ophelia
(how we love to adorn masks to hide our trauma)
i chose toxic love injections over the mirror
(a woman's first mistake is putting herself second)

i admit i'm a little messed up
(but doesn't alice say all the best people are?)
society exhausts me pretending they're not
(the world's a stage and i quit playing)
this is all of me,
perfectly flawed.

IN BETWEEN THEN AND NOW

a rusted gate rises from my embers
obscuring the old me in murky memories
blips of an aged silent film
where color is unattainable
and my laughter
carries no sound

i reach through the corroded
fence and my eyes bear witness
to my phantom self across
the graveyard, who waves from her
ghostly perch on the bed
where it all happened

even when i see all my abandoned traits
etched in cracked headstones and
the black widows whisper my secrets
this haunt no longer taunts me

because with medusa's pain
i morphed into a serpent
who sheds her skin in order
to flourish, instead of turning
my heart to stone

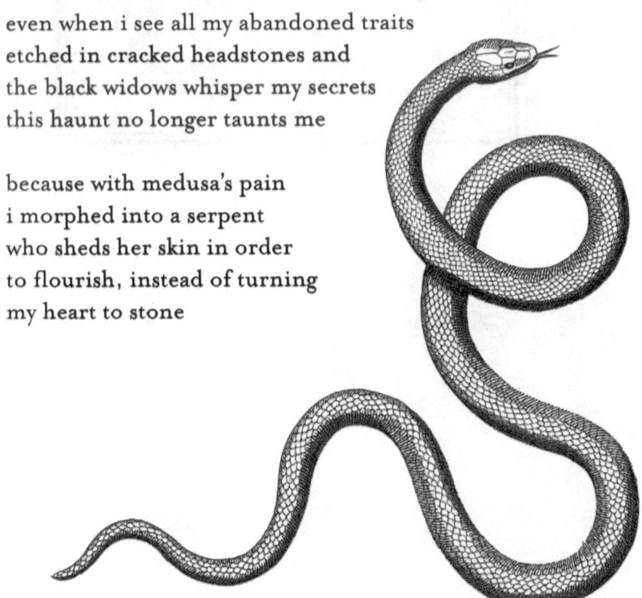

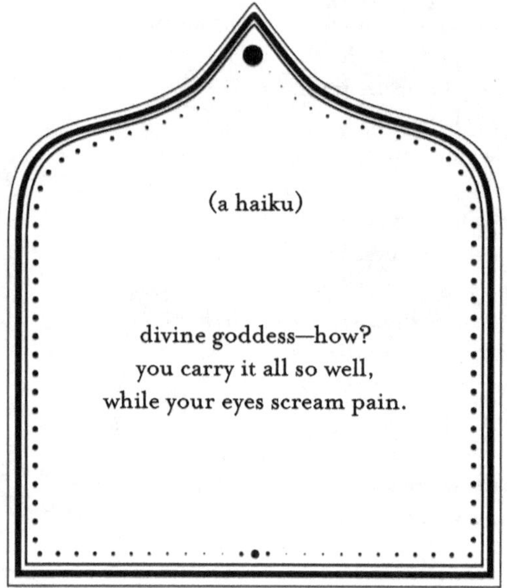

(a haiku)

divine goddess—how?
you carry it all so well,
while your eyes scream pain.

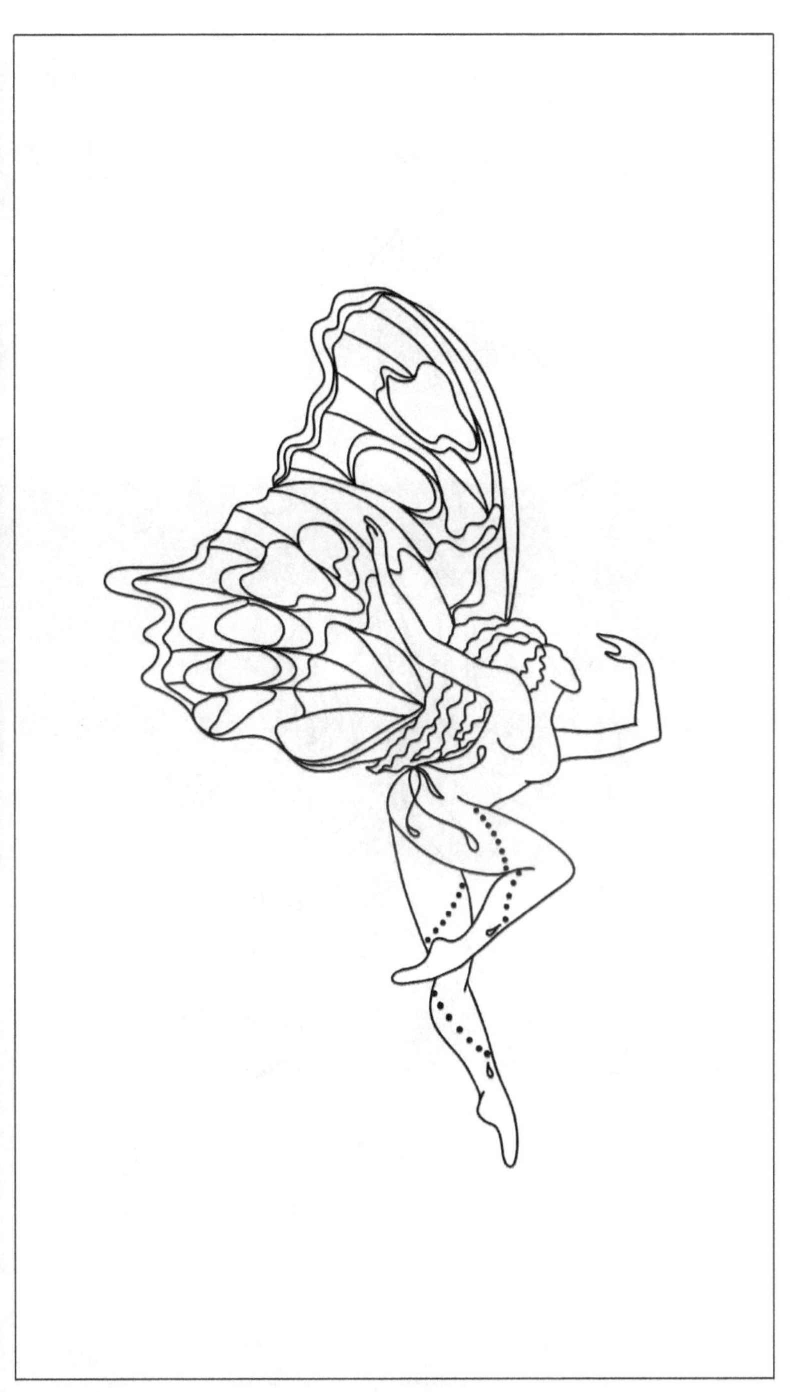

AURORA

a sting of fresh morning air
bypasses the flesh
and nestles into my bones
blankets are not enough
to warm this vessel my soul is tied to
but i sit outside and listen to the birds
gossip at the top of the trees
the foliage waves to me
with the help of the wind

i am aurora in the evergreen forest
looking for herself instead of a prince

grieving on a sunny day
praying for a glimmer of god
to beam and burrow into my skin
seep deep in my tissue and trickle
down my bones, soak in my bloodstream;

bless life into this numb body of mine.

LEGACY

paint my body
in ancient art
fill my mind with fables
in aged storybooks
time travel through
each crooning vinyl

**my muse knew my idols
she warns me**
"you can do it too"

i need to sit in the rawness
bury myself in my murky waters
trust my soul will reincarnate
and bloom into a lotus

you see, i'm a Holy Woman
and some days i'm an Angry Woman
and some days i'm a Crazy Woman
and yet my light beams through the very pores
that breathe life in and out of me,
because purity does not necessarily mean
a white gown and false promises before your god
but a pureness of soul, an authenticity of soul,
that includes both the glorious fruit and rotten decay
you see, my flaws make me a Powerful Woman
for how could i learn to stand again
if i never fall?

EDEN'S TREE

i stand before eden's tree
feel eve twitch in my bones
i wipe blood off my mouth
my rage erupts in black crows
i wonder when hate for women
was planted or how such a sin
could even grow

portals to beyond
yet we're blamed
for apple eating?

i conjure violet flames
let fury weep down my skin
let it be known, their sacrilege
rots our fruit from within

when i incinerate eden to ashes
i bathe in revenge's sweet inferno
as the devil,
      what wicked envy,
           lies bare and exposed

SPIRIT

spirit

what is spirit?

the very essence of you.
    the very essence of me.

it's everything we can and cannot see.

the circle of life, the higher self – spirit is eternity.

spirit weaves into earth tides, our sacred connection between
body and moon. spirit is radiant aura, feathery angel wings, the
soft budding of a newborn flower and the orange death of a falling
leaf. spirit is the embryo and the grave, the hushed ghost over your
shoulder, the fresh meadow my soul seeks during meditation, the
starlight tiptoeing in winter's frosty window.

spirit is faith as i surrender to life's inevitable flow and flexibility.
spirit is knowing this earthly home is temporary but i carry the
beginning of time in my veins.

i trust i've been here before. i trust i'll be back again.

my spirit smiles, guides me, reminds me –
you are both angel and human.
you are air, water, fire, and earth.
you are stars and endless space
all at once.

REINCARNATION

my soul washes up on shore
spent, light, shedding a lifetime
off its shoulders, letting it fall,
like a silk cloak brushing
against marble floor

i cleanse in fire, rain, sea salt,
gasping as each element caresses
my human wounds, each time
             holding space

i am drunk in my humanness
even my soul's dark, damp echoes
i weep, a ghost, my past now
a blip of a fever dream—

i ache for all the times
i railed against life; oh,
but if i can,
      i will do it all
           again.

THANK YOU

a huge thank you to my partner and my coven for being forever
supportive of my creative writing journey (and me!).
i love you all so much and this book
would not be here without your loving support.

thank you to shelby leigh for the terrific edits and
encouraging comments on my manuscript. thank you to r. clift
for the gorgeous cover and book design, and bringing my ideas
to life.

thank you, mother earth, and miss moon,
for your endless life and tides.

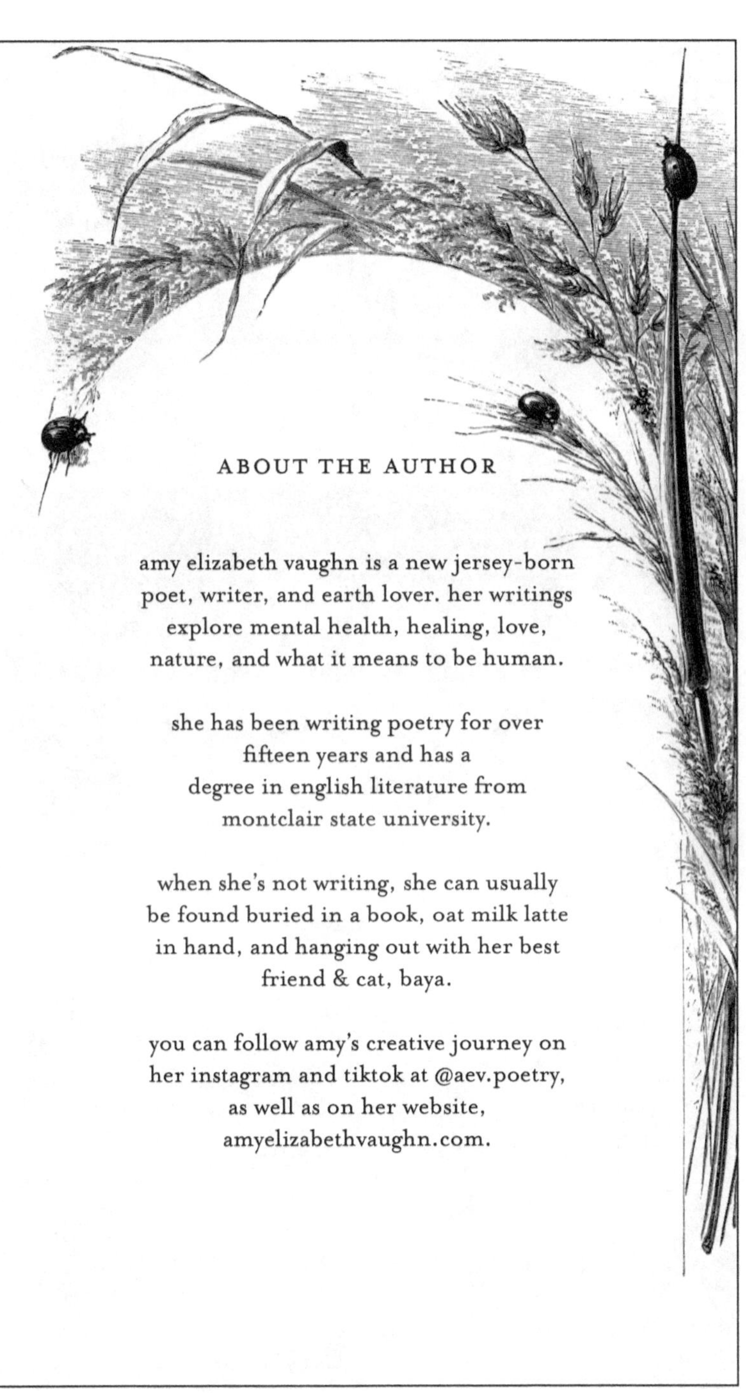

ABOUT THE AUTHOR

amy elizabeth vaughn is a new jersey-born
poet, writer, and earth lover. her writings
explore mental health, healing, love,
nature, and what it means to be human.

she has been writing poetry for over
fifteen years and has a
degree in english literature from
montclair state university.

when she's not writing, she can usually
be found buried in a book, oat milk latte
in hand, and hanging out with her best
friend & cat, baya.

you can follow amy's creative journey on
her instagram and tiktok at @aev.poetry,
as well as on her website,
amyelizabethvaughn.com.

NOTES

i'm forever inspired by my muses – mother earth, quiet galleries filled with enchanting brushstrokes, galaxies, fairytales sleeping in bookshelves, and most often, my fellow artists. i'm blessed to be surrounded and inspired by so many great creative children of earth, past generations and present.

thank you to the below creatives who inspired my own light with their lovely prompts and artwork.

escapril 2023 (@letsescapril)
> *prompts: 'a bit of advice' (page 11); 'a vision of the future' (page 28); 'skin' (page 34); 'synapses' (page 82); 'blush' (page 89); 'attention' (page 91).*

medha (@medhaawrites)
> *after medha's poem, 'my recent google searches' (page 13).*

william shakespeare

kamakshi anand (@wingedwords02)
> *prompts: 'muse' and 'the ghosts have gone home' (page 18); 'spirits rose one last time' and 'this is the language of grievers' (page 56).*

isabel rocio (@isabelrocio_)
> *after isabel rocio's poem, 'when you ask me why i write poetry' (page 25).*

madeleine watts
> *first line 'for my — for the thing i had lost' taken from madeleine watts's book 'the inland sea' (page 41).*

lois rose (@lrsterlingpoetry)
> *prompt: 'my junk drawer is full, tell me where to put my pain' (page 66).*

shannon e. stephan (@writtenbyshannon)
> *after shannon e. stephan's poem, 'you ask me about my first love' (page 90).*

elena riccardini (@elliepoetry_)
> *prompts: 'strums my vocal chords,' 'discolor my lips,' and 'take a slice of my madness' (page 100).*

noelle darilek (@noellewritespoetry)
> *prompt: 'lava dripping down your skin' (page 103).*

snoh aalegra

ana (@the_artsy_writer) & sara catherine (@saracatherinepoetry)
> *prompts: 'the skin you see me wearing isn't mine' and 'i must weed out the demons in my coffin before i sleep' (page 138).*

frank ocean
> *inspired by frank ocean lyric 'glimmer of god' (page 144).*

kehlani parrish
> *inspired by 'intro' on sweetsexysavage album (page 147).*